VISITANTS

John Kinsella: bibliography

BOOKS

The Frozen Sea (Zeppelin Press, 1983)
The Book of Two Faces (PICA, 1989)
Night Parrots (Fremantle Arts Centre Press, 1989)
Eschatologies (FACP, 1991)
Full Fathom Five (FACP, 1993)
Syzygy (FACP, 1993)
The Silo: A Pastoral Symphony (FACP, 1995; Arc, UK, 1997)
Erratum/ Frame(d) (Folio/FACP, 1995)
The Radnoti Poems (Equipage, UK, 1996)
Anathalamion (Poetical Histories, UK, 1996)
The Undertow: New & Selected Poems (Arc, UK, 1996)
Lightning Tree (FACP, 1996)
Graphology (Equipage, UK, 1997)
Genre (prose fiction, FACP, 1997)
Poems 1980-1994 (FACP, 1997; Bloodaxe Books, 1998)
The Hunt and other poems (FACP/Bloodaxe Books, 1998)
Grappling Eros (stories, FACP, 1998)
The Kangaroo Virus Project, with Ron Sims (Folio/FACP, 1998)
Visitants (Bloodaxe Books/FACP, 1999)

AS EDITOR

The Bird Catcher's Song (Salt, 1992)
A Salt Reader (Folio/Salt, 1995)
Poetry (Chicago) – double issue of Australian poetry
    (with Joseph Parisi, USA, 1996)
Landbridge: Contemporary Australian Poetry (FACP/Arc, 1999)

VISITANTS

JOHN KINSELLA

BLOODAXE BOOKS

ISBN: 1 85224 505 0

First published 1999 by
Bloodaxe Books Ltd,
P.O. Box 1SN,
Newcastle upon Tyne NE99 1SN.

Bloodaxe Books Ltd acknowledges
the financial assistance of Northern Arts.

Cover printing by J. Thomson Colour Printers Ltd, Glasgow.

Printed in Great Britain by
Cromwell Press Ltd, Trowbridge, Wiltshire.

for Marjorie Perloff

'Think about that. The receptiveness. So many visitants coming, none that anyone knows of ever driven away.'
— RANDOLPH STOW

Acknowledgements

Acknowledgements are due to the editors of the following publications where some of these poems first appeared: *Kenyon Review, London Review of Books, New Blood* (Bloodaxe Books, 1999), *Overland, Poetry London Newsletter, Nimrod, Recursive Angel, The Rialto, Southerly, Sulfur, Thumbscrew, Tinfish, Times Literary Supplement, Varuna New Poetry* and *Verse*.

The poems 'Aspects of the Pagan' and 'Akbar' are taken from *The Radnoti Poems* (Equipage, Cambridge, 1997) and 'Beyond W. Eugene Smith's Photographic Essay *Life Without Germs*' from *Erratum/Frame(d)* (Folio/FACP, 1995). The poems 'Down off the shoulder of the pink granite scarp' and 'Divining' were abducted from my play *Crop Circles*.

Contents

ASPECTS OF THE PAGAN

MAKING CONTACT

A Bright Cigar-Shaped Object Hovers
Over Mount Pleasant

It starts in the park near Brentwood Primary School
and moves rapidly towards Mount Pleasant
a bright cigar-shaped object that darts
and jolts across the demarcation lines
of class that aren't supposed to exist in Australia
but do because even Labor voters prefer
to be on the Mount Pleasant side of the divide
if for no other reason than it pushes property
prices up. It follows the line of my escape-
route from school, the same route a man
without a face in a dark car crawls along,
calling to me as I break into a run,
the car door opening and a clawed hand
reaching out to drag me in, the cigar-
shaped object stopped stock still
and hovering like the sun, hovering
as if it's always been in that spot, always
been overhead, as hot as hell despite
the cold setting in, the sweat emanating
from my forehead, the light bright in my eyes.

Phenomenology

'But with the advance of civilisation, this biology has become a problem.'
DONNA J. HARAWAY

1. *the dance – elusive gender*

My brother noticed them first – dancing
in the backyard of our quarter acre in the city.
On the lawn, under the golden wattle tree.
I said it had something to do with the telephone
system I'd rigged up between our neighbour's
house and ours. I talked to the kid next door
late at night. He was the kid that said if we
connected our cocks we'd get a charge.
They've been attracted by the power in the lines
I said – I've upset the balance. They danced
for hours every night, and my brother sat up
on his bed in the sleepout and watched
until he was dizzy. He was sick in the mornings
and when he told me what happened
I punched his arm. But I went in
some nights later and saw them too –
glowing figures with strange limbs
like Roswell aliens. We both
commented on their 'lack' and guessed
them to be girls. They stopped
coming or we grew bored and forgot
about them. The golden cypress
grew so tall a storm knocked its top off
and the telephone lines between my room
and the kid's next door were cut.

2. *sightings*

They passed over our house on a few occasions when I was a child. They apparently continued to do so but I stopped seeing them when I went to high school – in fact, I didn't even bother to look. On two occasions my mother reported them to the *West Australian* newspaper and the airforce base at Pearce and the next day the sightings were listed in the paper. My wife's family were doing the same thing. My wife's mother believed her children were from other planets. She wanted to take them to a commune in the hills to await the arrival of the mother ship. The sightings were always similar. What I remember is how they dazzled me, and how I got to stay up late.

3. *seeing*

I've written a poem about she-oaks
scratching at the windows
of that room at Wheatlands.
When I first read Frost
it was the birches that got me.
The ouija board came out
when the adults went to a show
in town and older cousins
were looking after us. The room
was dark and the blinds open
and there was a frost
on the ploughed fields.
The light was yellow
but no more than on
other clear nights
at that time of year.
The sheep huddled together
and the half-moon gouged
furrows into their stiff fleeces.
The wind – rising and falling –
drove she-oak needles
and upset the frost. Not quite
black but getting that way.
The board gave back my name
and I imagined myself dead.
I couldn't feel anything.
Said nothing. Years later
a friend pulled the death card
from a tarot pack.
That was a hot summer's evening
and the river was low
and smelt of decomposition.
His death came some time later.
He drowned in that river
and the coroner built
a psychological portrait
of a man who'd died
and returned.

4. *fruit*

My mother
knew a woman
who could make fruit
fly around a room.
If she stared
at a fruit bowl
long enough
it would explode.
She told my mother
about her family
and her life.
Things
my mother
already knew.
And she told her
how things
would be.

5. *keeping your mouth shut – against conspiracy*

Area-51 was a place called Nungalloo
just north of Geraldton. The huge
mineral sands processing plants
of Jennings and Allied mutated
out of borderline farmland.
As if a neutral zone, Associated Labs
sat nearby, upwind. Testing
monozite and rutile
late at night a storm hit
the narrative and the x-ray
equipment went wild, the gun
shooting rays outside its alignment,
the telex scripting the electric air,
my flesh spread like an internal horizon –
a chemiluminescent shadow puppet
experimenting with form,
my organs glowed and I watched
the machinery of my fear,
the production of silence.

'That's Venus?' the girl asked. 'It doesn't look like much.'

– FREDERIK POHL, *The Merchants of Venus*

The grass has gone. Gravel
fills in the blanks around
the rose beds. Somebody
snaps the heads of a thousand

agapanthus. You can see
something he can't. Woomera
kick-starts. Watering is limited
to two hours, after sunset

or at first light. Drought. Apollo –
a mining entrepreneur, or the lights of Perth.
Lights out. Calling occupants. He baulks
and Barbarella skips a pleasure pill.

He claims you're making it up.
And is convinced early on. You're twelve.
At twenty, the ships are silver-skinned
and glowing. They wear the cloak

of authenticity – well travelled.
In and out of the garden year after year.
Through puberty, into his old age –
his very old age. Klaatu's peace gesture

collapses like a car smash
on a nearby corner. An eclipse
brings silence and children
grow slowly blind. He's muttering,

and you say they're very close.
Hot and close. Venus is a hot planet –
once they thought it a second earth.
The cloud feigns atmosphere

and drought doesn't require
hot weather. You doubt what you see
but don't let on. Time's jumping about.
You install reticulation. He keeps

off the gravel – irregular
ochre ball-bearings, like oxidised tinfoil
collected in wads to help a war effort,
disappearing into the furnace.

They come when you're asleep,
get into your brain,
hijack your faculties.
You're never the same person

when you wake up. Someone new
in there every night. Morning.
Grids. Timetables. The powder burns
that heal like paper cuts.

You draw pictures – intricate diagrams;
translate alien technologies.
A nightbird settles in the eaves.
It's silent, like Pine Gap.

He takes a transistor radio
into Church to get the scores –
the same minister will say the rites.
You've genetically modified your soul.

It attaches itself to the nearest object
as the body's on its way out.
You see Venus – it doesn't look like much.
The roses are ordinary.

The House: Progress, the Paranormal, and a Sighting

Your house mesmerised with its portico
and bay windows and floating tableau of sheet metal
rising in peaks and troughs, intensified
by the threshold between the sea's white-light
running widdershins in the tidal rush
and an off-centre and elongated vista,
focussing the town or feigning
an aura or intensifying the sibilant flights
of sea-birds or those birds for which the proximity
of the sea is not unfamiliar –
their presence a syllogism
for sensitivity to the Other Side,
the ad-hoc or stand-in medium,
impresario of otherness.
When an observation or *encounter*
caught in your throat and gagged
like conspiracy, as The Shadow ran down the corridor
and you measured ectoplasm by the millilitre,
weighed probability on a Mettler balance,
put the perspiration that appeared
on your forehead – it being high summer –
to the spectrograph; and as door handles turned
at night and the verandahs seemed
to grip the field of the house even closer
you thought of your mother
teaching English to the prisoners
across the street, the limestone and red brick
of the old hospital your home contracting
with macro abruptness, the off-sea wind
driving hard against the fever,
turning it to powder.

From the inside looking out,
you revelled in the apprehension
of passers-by: 'Who'd live in the old hospital
with its heritage of agues and premature deaths?'
saying over to yourself that it was the decay
outside that drove the sickness here.

From above, the settlement looks like a dot painting
of the chaos theory, the electric clocks
in the house crazy, light on the windows
buzzing like foo fighters over a chromium sea; history
is your recollection, and years later a car park
and shopping centre will seal the troubled
airs within, the sea still glinting, photographs
of the 'old place' – incidents
glaring like exposure.

Mesmerised

My brother fixated
on the eclipse
and outside consequence
had 20-20 vision.
Outside science
he remains mesmerised
by the vagaries
of the sun,
the moon's moodiness.
I, obscured by logic
and a knowledge
of the eye
kept my gaze
averted, or fixed
on the image
as translated
by a pinhole camera.
Now I struggle to see
even the darkest shadow
closing over me,
sensing rather
its coolness
its power
to do damage.
The sun burns,
the moon is cold,
the planets orbit
indifferently.

Child Sightings

Out there the skies were wide
and shooting stars would come
on clear nights, and showers of light
would fill the summer air.
Sometimes I'd watch from my room
as they came down
and lit up fields, as bright as fire
though nothing caught.
I'd reach out through the glass.
After they came, I'd stay silent
watching and talking to them
inside my brain. At first I was scared
and wanted to scream, but nothing
happened, like in a dream. Then
I just gave in and wasn't afraid.
People tell me now
the wheatbelt is full of phenomena
that might be explained:
ball lightning, Jack-o'-lanterns,
meteorite showers.
I used to squeeze my eyes
tight to make colours come,
spin in circles until I fell
or hold my breath until stars vanished
and there was nothing, nothing
just as they claim.

Alienation

'*Curiously enough, in the conditions in which someone says to you,*
freedom or death! *the only proof of freedom that you can have in
the conditions laid out before you is precisely to choose death,
for there, you show that you have freedom of choice.*'
JACQUES LACAN OR JACQUES-ALAIN MILLER?

In the phone tap the poison gets out
beamed down or fed into the machine,
encrypted as language
you can hear them speak,
watch them think in the fuzz
of the television screen,
the station out and the tube
pulling their bitter rubbish in –
the lethal factor: transfixed
it's so loud the electric haze
spreads its shadow
through your limbs, filling
each cell to the point of burning.
A group of sufferers meet
in the hills of suburban Perth,
they know the proof is death,
the aliens eating flesh,
eating their stomachs
from the inside out –
the group as collective defence,
their mantra: 'freedom is death'.
I come to this. A cousin's
mother-in-law asks me
to tune her short-wave radio
into the BBC World Service,
almost. Just off-frequency,
you can hear them speak.
It's almost English.
Not written down, it's told
a different way each time.

The punctuation fluctuates,
free-falling through a home video,
memories of a particular
wedding anniversary.
Your money or your life!
Don't dress fancy, they look
for difference. Separation
and othering makes you receptive.
She says this after death – a letter
explaining her silence.
The cancer biopsied and kept
in storage. One devotee down
the group heats up,
develops a sense of urgency:
surfing the net, awaiting
the Terror, the devolutionary pop groups,
body piercings, dance drugs,
freedom of choice.

Rites of Harvest

In deadwood
or on ropes of haze,
suspended
in brittle air
the parrots shimmer
brightly –
          they hear
your determined steps
across the vacant
paddocks,
          the crunch of salt
below your boots.

I place my hands
to the surface
of ouija night
& write landfill
& title deeds
like premonitions
across the deck
of wet hessian
that covers
the silo's bare floor.
Without map
or advice
I set out with you
across the salt,
never doubting
the accuracy of your step,
the rites
of harvest.

The Plinth that Haunts the Photograph
A Hoax?

I'd swear it wasn't there before I lifted
the camera – a Pentax Super – I looked
directly at what's now the picture.
And I'm looking at it now – that *2001*-like plinth
rising out of the field, defying
sky and fenceline and bales of leaden cloud.
Maybe the eye is slower
than the one on sixty time imposed upon the scene?
The plinth appearing like disaster.
A dark object that's in reality
all glare – tinted glasses
as black as the eye of a deep and dying well.
But this is no shady
interpolation like those made
of extraterrestrials or beasts
in Loch Ness, snapped with distorting
filters, touched up in dark-rooms.
No, it's too clear. Though I suppose
it may have been a flaw in the film,
or the maker's name imposed
during manufacture. A hoax
replicated in every snap –
watermarks in a ream
of high quality paper,
every square nanometre
a grave.

Take care in the long grass

Take care in the long grass
the long dry summer grass
in this zone of dugites and gwarders
even a stray tiger snake
take care your gaiters
are strapped tight
or that denim is double-thickness
and tucked tight into boot tops
bridled with burrs,
resistant to the strike,
latch and puncture,
hot as hell sweating, prickling
and saying damn-it-all, give me thongs,
and a tourniquet and a bottle of Condy's Crystals
and a mouth that'll suck venom
out like death IS love; long grass rustling
brittle fabric like wings on insects
enough to lift you out of the thick of it,
high as the soul need go
to escape dugite, gwarder,
errant tiger snake out from the dank
fringe of swamp,
the long grass,
the nomenclature of poison
and body

A THEORY OF FORMS

The Three Laws of Robotics

*1. A robot may not injure a human being, or, through
inaction, allow a human being to come to harm.*
*2. A robot must obey the orders given it by human beings
except where such orders would conflict with the First Law.*
*3. A robot must protect its own existence as long as such
protection does not conflict with the First or Second Law.*

— Handbook of Robotics, 56th Edition, 2058 A.D., *I, Robot*

The iron man
from the North
attacks Aborigines
and gloats in his pub
and there's no surprise
in the ministerial banks
and the press
swivels on its monopoly
satellite precise
paparazzi positronic Robbie
robopsychology
fundamentalist
neighbours packing up
and heading for the city
where bright lights
obscure and contradict
sightings – radioactive tailings
bringing a glow
to their gardens.
Mother so wanted to believe
in the signifying craft,
the One to which all others
would call in time of need,
the warm singularity.
We drive on the left-hand
side of the road.
We import heavy equipment,
OD on nostalgia.
"Japanese" is repellently attractive –
bigotry is taking the investment
and publishing snide cartoons,
lampooning the hand that feeds

pig-iron bob and the court of jesters,
yes, the black arm-band generation,
yes the defacement of Eddie Mabo
by right-wing robots who wouldn't hurt
their parliamentary makers,
and Blainey out there touting
his sense of "history" –
searching out
illegal aliens,
hardcore porn
brought in on boats
through Geraldton harbour,
speed factories in the offices
of multinational companies,
the sell the sell the sell
storing identity, dragging power
out of the forbidden country
like mind control, and Uri Geller
converting the abundant
Westralian sunshine
to the stuff of referenda,
bending odes to the Conservation Minister.
Given heart, the US company
might dump its nuclear wastes
in "our" open spaces –
a company video crows.
Or elsewhere, fighter bombers
losing missiles and generals
giving up on the idea
of collateral damage.
The cost the cost the cost.
Alive or dead, it's a target.
The organic view of a mechanised society –
all are culpable. Assassination
like pyramid selling.
War poets don't quite know
what to do with clichés
and the robot prime minister
contradicts the first law
and then looks to having
it changed in parliament.
The Guardian backs him to the hilt.

He modifies all three laws
and calls in more Harriers –
flying missions despite the weather –
the pressures of the market economy.
It's called the Westminster system.
Bill Gates wants in to my computer.
It's called a treaty, or a "defence pact".
The Atlantic is merely a puddle
full of oil and fallout.
This is what they mean by the lyrical I.
The human may not injure
the robot, the police
make sure of this.

Skylab and the Theory of Forms

(for Jeremy Prynne)

We didn't make it but we ended up getting it,
or parts of it at least. I've seen chunks
and my wife's father brought some home
for them as kids. In the tradition
of those splinters of the True Cross
held in reliquaries around the world,
if you added all the chunks
together there'd have been an entire
city in space. There's a novel simmering
in its iconic resonance, the charred black
remains the talisman that starts
or in the very least attracts a cult.
Like the Aum Supreme Truth Cult,
that had a place out there, somewhere
where the land is less fertile and not so
closely scrutinised. Members may
not have known about Skylab
but the prospect of the world
crashing down on their neighbours
would have spurred them on.
But Skylab's not like them,
nor like the couple from the Subcontinent
who named their newborn in its honour,
being American it's as good as having
Elvis or Marilyn paraphernalia dropped
in your back yard. People pay
good money for stuff like this.
Kids of my generation remember
the diagrams in magazines
and newspapers. The neat bodies
of astronauts suspended in the neat
compartments. Small had great potential.
And it looked much more modern
than anything the Ruskies
could put up there. But maybe now
we can see that such assumptions
were merely a matter of taste.

Soviet Space Trash is also
worth a fortune, and promises
the exotic in the subtext
of THE modern novel. A kind of
accidental empire building,
an occupation of the vacant spaces.
Like Woomera. A roar that fills
the void of Terra Nullius.

Sparklers, Hawks, & Electric Trains

The magnetic float
stylised
like in-form critics
plundering
sure bets
through respectable
media outlets.
Rolf Harris's stylophone
humms, whizzes, and buzzes
like a conspiracy
brewed in caves deep
beneath the Nullarbor Plain.
Which has something
to do with Americans.
The evidence:
a photograph,
fuzzy around the edges.
The electric train glides   .
silently
out of the station
and nails a dozen pedestrians
slickly to the sleepers.
The high voltage lines
hover overhead
like inimitable hawks.
Nobody can work them out.
But then sparklers
shape-shifting
in rail-side
backyards
divine
a brilliant future.
That much
          at least
is clear.

Immaterial Objectives

(for Martin Leer)

> *'No, UFOs aren't a big thing in Denmark. People are more concerned*
> *with material things. They don't want to miss out on owning something.*
> *And material in the sense that they believe entirely in their bodies. They*
> *spend a lot of money on exercise equipment – you know, torture machines.*
> *UFOs seem to belong more to cultures disturbed by spiritual uncertainty,*
> *or paranoia. Or societies riddled with guilt. Or a dissatisfaction with*
> *the material conditions of their existence. A place in crisis like the US or*
> *Britain fits the bill perfectly. And so would Australia, in parts, as well.'*

They jogged out and over the city limits,
crossing the frontier. The city lights persisted
and the night sky remained partially obscured.
The pumping action of their legs drove pheromones
from somewhere – Reeboks are an out-of-body
experience if the leaps of Michael Jordan
are to be believed. Small animals long thought
extinct followed in their wake. They glowed
like radiation. And as the bitumen turned
to gravel the phosphorescence of their foot-
prints lingered, like krill brilliant in the most
vibrant of oceans. Sweating it out they forgot
why they were running. It was as if a huge load
was lifted from their shoulders. Returning along
the same path they became disorientated,
the glow rapidly fading, the animals going,
the city a memory from which this frontier
was constructed, this other empire of the senses.

Dispossession

WATSON: *Where do wicked people go at death?*
YEENAR: *To a very great fire I believe.*
WATSON: *That is very bad, and is not to be trifled with.*
YEENAR: O*h yes fire very good, very good.*

> Journal of W. Watson, 21 September 1834,
> Church Missionary Society Records, AJCP.

protection
aggravated
destruction
Almighty
construction
proclamation
probability
autonomy
disease
species
autonomy
links
quality
vis-à-vis
the centralised
London dealer in native art
landing
like something out of songlines
the press
commission/s
traditional
punishments
appropriate
authentic
threads
heresy
controls
white hunters
alcohol
abuse
custody

motivating
sit-down
leaders
nominated
by
mining companies
pastoral leases
progressive
impacts
and sustain
extinguishment!
as assistance
modifies acts
presence
traces
the local
and maintains
representatives
authentic
claims
to constitutional
strategy
faith
and ownership
rifles
revisionist
histories: lights
in the sky
shackles

High Noon – A Visitation

(after Edward Hopper)

The prospect of his return is tenuous
though she persists as the sun's
high overhead and he always comes
out of the sun, cloaked in light.
But as she stands in the door frame,
transfixed by hum of summer, the chevron
of roof-shadow threatens like the umbra
of a sundial or malignant planet,
and the chinks in the curtains
ache like the blue of the broad sky.
As the glasses clink in a distant hotel
she'll clutch her blue peignoir close to her breast,
growing increasingly conscious of her nakedness,
telling herself that the nothingness
of the open space that surrounds the house
is an illusion, that when the rains come
it will be rich with flowers, that the green
pasture will be her refuge.

On Lucas van Valckenborch's *La Tour de Babel*

(for John Tranter)

Though not quite the World Trade Center
or Sears tower there is a touch of vertigo
about it, and certainly a sense
that symmetry and precision
are part of the system, that the universe
is ordered and measurable;
that if finished
the tower would reach Heaven,
because its distance from Earth
is exact if one calculates
all ascensions from sea level.
Were we able to find
a constant in perspective,
we could deduce
whether Babel would have required
an aerial or lightning conductor
mounted on top
of the observation platform
to pierce the floor of Heaven,
had not the builders been struck down
and language made victim,
cast out as an imperfect
and dangerous science.

The Savagery of Birds

As smog drifts up from the city
you realise that the sky is really
a painted backdrop, and Nature
has no part in it, that all around
you is construct – the silos,
the sheds, the tractors, the trucks,
cybernetic animals wearing
fashionable genes, mechanical
birds that fly with the gravity
and grace of a computer simulation
while wearing expressions that belong
to mythology, making Frans Snyders's
Oiseaux sur des branches relevant
to the end of the twentieth century,
to a place deep down in the South,
where grain-eating birds are turning
to flesh that tastes like muesli.

Untitled

or the use of the word 'it'

> *'The work which established Hirst's reputation in the British art world is
> entitled "The Physical Impossibility of Death in the Mind of Someone
> Living" (Pl.324). It consists of a dead tiger shark floating in a tank of
> preservative fluid. The shark has been balanced and weighted so that
> it floats in the middle of its tank, just as though it were floating in
> its natural element.'*
>
> EDWARD LUCIE-SMITH, *Artoday*

Its tank is as
an emerald and chilled sea,
drenched in protean light,
its gut filled with the leaden boots
of a lost solo circumnavigator,
tropical conjuring
of the Other,
in this Albion, this island state
as rare as uniqueness
or that *perfect* steak,
that attracted language-wise
and even geographically
Joseph Conrad,
and islanders such as myself
who know that sharks
can't afford to miss a beat –
drowning a threat to the machine that drives
their jaws, like art
and patronage
and representation: not the life-mechanism
but the weighting of a non-expanding universe;
hey, Damien, maybe
you've backed the wrong shark?
'It' the elemental nature, O
composited artist
of the dead, as if it belongs
to its own patch of turf,
the flesh advertised
(Saatchi Collection)
like a tiger consuming villagers

and being shot
out of "necessity", its skin
elemental in its stately spread,
trophy with unique
life-giving properties,
a comfort to the living,
O enfant terrible,
provocateur,
bête noire
ad infinitum, fluid

BODY SNATCHING

Failing the Personality Test

Clawed-in recruitment material
lingering doubts co-opted, hi-jacked
by clean sorts with nice teeth,
the stench of piss or drink
but youthful enough to go the distance,
attitude acceptable as it might signify strength,
always make good foot soldiers;
better still – golden recruits – clean shirts, cuffs
and collars and a very small mobile
telephone, couples entirely appropriate,
in the pink of life, the Saab, late model
Japanese vehicles okay; a touch of sex
but it won't exist outside the clique,
and then the genepool is tightly controlled;
so, having agreed to the text, your rage
might drop you into subpar aggressive
tendencies, no hope of repair, unclean,
unprofitable, too well read and not well
read enough, a piece of apocryphal
detritus, beyond the council,
the stratagems of eternal recruitment,
for whom there'll never be a Master,
just murky suspicions and guesswork

Body Snatching

(for Elizabeth Grosz)

*'The phantom is an expression of nostalgia for the unity and
wholeness of the body, its completion. It is a memorial to the
missing limb, a psychical delegate that stands in its place. There
is thus not only a physical but also a psychical wound and scar
in the amputation or surgical intervention into any part
of the body. The phantom limb is the narcissistic reassertion
of the limb's presence in the face of its manifest biological loss,
an attempt to preserve the subject's narcissistic sense of bodily
wholeness (an image, as Lacan points out, developed through
the mirror stage).'*

ELIZABETH GROSZ, Volatile Bodies

1

Wearing her family tree like an extra limb
she made hay while the sun shone –
on the couch, in the face of disaster,
she sang lullabies, as if the world
were her baby. The group's collective energy
shone like a halo and kept the Others out.
Birds erupted from her fingertips,
swamps dried out in her presence.
The ooze retreated somewhere
between a rock and a hard place,
vaporised in the slow undulations of the valley
as supple orifices of planting
steeled themselves against seed-drill,
pod, the vegetable body that replicates
and moves on emotionless, like a trick
of perpetuation mirrored and delegated "family",
the genealogical quirk: she sensed an outerbody,
the shell of her grandmother, entrapment
of an earlier self: whom can we trust
if not the doctors, our relatives?

2

He articulated as if his voice should carry
a specific weight, presence like volume
that'd fill the room: a projection
like the mise en scène that is the interior
of his tractor's cabin (his pride and joy,
an almost new John Deere). The plough's hyperbole
upturning relics where there are none to be found,
the primary cultures not building durably,
just traces – carbon copies of an earlier draft.
The yields are expected to be higher than ever.

3

In the hothouse they're all incestuous.
Fluid is more readily retained.
It is conducive to recycling.
Biosphere. Micro homunculi magnified big
and transplanted into casual conversation.
Like a wig. Or an encounter with angel hair.
The whole family was welcome at the gathering.
Waterbirds filled the driest places.

4

She specifically laid herself out
for his scrutiny. He examined the base of the limb
and declared its width a travesty. There was
no precedent. The first rains came at the right time.
But they continued unabated and the topsoil
ran reddish brown into the creeks, down to the river.
Distantly, the estuaries choked and fishermen
lamented the lack of sport. They formed pressure groups.
They believed not only the weather was to blame.

5.

Flowdown stigmata as if vocation or vision
or being struck down at the bus stop are only excrescence;
occupying the same body space, synchro reflex
actions, as if walking towards an end,
picaresque or screen print, centrefold spread
and the whole lot leaking out through the staple holes:
legible handwriting had them saying
he writes with a feminine hand,
recording the exact dimensions of the bald domed heads
belonging to his abductors, the beauty
of the Darling Ranges
in Spring roneo'd over and over again.

The Bermuda Triangle

Pat Rafter, saviour of Australian tennis,
maintains a comfortable existence on Bermuda;
the flight of balls determined by the weather,
which island-culture makes more tropical
than it should – the concentration of emptiness
and expectation like nationalism postponed
and sent offshore – the Queen's English
an experimental turn of phrase on the front
doorstep of liberty, the fraternal vanishings
of flight on flight of the right stuff, as if Play-
Station IS living, as if a package holiday
has you hungering after the wealth
of the pyramids, concentrated to an echoing
point of ambiguity, like the limitations
of radar, and re-runs of *The Day the Earth
Stood Still* – remaining black and white
as childhood – making an ocean of the river,
the bright ship whispering through the ever
widening hole in the ozone layer.

Beyond W. Eugene Smith's Photographic Essay
Life Without Germs
(*Life*, 26 September 1949)

A research facility called 'Lobund' shrouded
in a night we guess is perpetual, the architecture
crematory, though not incendiary – a dark foreboding rot-
down may spark, fill the chamber, and catch the suited alien
unawares, a representative of the human species
seeking to penetrate the mystery behind the thickened glass.

A Bela Lugosi leer, and not before time, the glass
eye of the microscope masking the light source, the shrouded
cell budding or mutating or both: foetus of a contrived species
devastated by routine conjecture, the shattered architecture
of its pre-life fed like the lay photographer or the alien
with whatever information they've got to spare; whatever rot.

Flesh absorbs in the harsh light, the residue or rot
of an experiment (a success we should gather), the glass
of the test-tube marked by the tip of a nail, the control alien
in its purity, though over-exposure deceives: shrouded,
the truth lies packed in trays of the just-born, an architecture
absorbed by that of the chamber, by the decreation of a species.

Compare the moral beauty of the rat and the face of a species
hidden behind a suit and a mask, that of a monkey and the rot
filling creases of guilt sculpted from rubber, the architecture
of iron, wheel valves, and gaskets, the portholes of glass
constantly resisting face-presses from stiffly shrouded
creatures that reek of B-Grade Sci-Fi horror flicks: alien.

The hand that reaches into the core of its being is alien
to itself: in the House of Usher the monkey reclines, a species
separated though connected for the duration of its shrouded
life with data accumulated by its peers. Its veins may rot
but its eyes remain stoical if apprehensive, their glass
sheen more dignified than the eyeless rat's fallen architecture.

Before opening the envelope that speaks the architecture
of the surface must be exposed cleanly, a discovery is alien
and as such must be revealed within the clarity of glass
and not obscured by extras (hair, fur, flesh). The species
of germ observed, removed, stored, and labelled, the rot
of the host's body is discarded. Even the living are shrouded.

The architecture of body and tomb will vary between species,
whether germ, animal, or alien – it's a fact that rot
obscures experimental glass, that a world germ-free is shrouded.

Area-51/Pine Gap – A Pastoral Romance

(for Nigel Wheale)

Bob Lazar – young scientist outdoing
Galileo and Church – back engineering
alien technology 37 light years from Zeta 2 Reticuli –
where fleece was removed lighter than air
crazy with killing hermaphrodites
like the FBI down here, covering
open spaces, quickly clearing 38
levels above theory, hoodwinking
physicists at Area-51,
which we pass through on the way to something
more glamorous: S-4 in Nevada,
Alamos National Laboratories,
telephone directories in Los Angeles–
Bob Lazar, youthful scientist – Majestic!
in the goldfields of Western Australia,
so hot it cooks the brains of jackeroos
trapping sheep by fencing off water,
leaving a narrow opening,
carcasses filling the wastes,
erased by amplifying gravity waves
and our love for Leon – poor shepherd
as cyborg unicorns procreate
in paper, origami signifying
sexual gravity A and sexual gravity B
in the genital [pocket].

The Nullarbor reverberates, the car radio
furious as static probes its brains,
the agathon propulsion system
the antimatter reactor, straited sphere
size of a medicine ball
fuelled by shepherdesses Clorin
and Cloe-on-pentium, periodic
replications, consorting
and saying love is nothing
but blood pressed against the ventricle edifice
mixing high in ambient lushness
of blood, the vascular hum – subterranean
as grass-eaters flow out and creatures
reject spiritual mass with a secular ease,
vultures and parrots flaking in the appalling light –
bombarded with protons, converting matter
into dirge of energy, hairs of wheat-lips
hanging in theatre like hypochondria:
signifying product and "epiphanic insights"

Weapons – essentially stable – target
the chromosomes of Seneca, attach transparent waves
of immigration to Pine Gap, the NRA,
Pauline Hanson, ASIO, *Sixty Minutes*
The White Australia Policy, advertising agencies,
gravity amplifiers, stones dropped in water-troughs
brimful with supernatural agency,
Rachel – glory of the Tyrrell corporation,
dams and waterholes and anywhere else
where the name of the family dwells:
they are without discretion.

Three hollow tubes
two feet in diameter
four feet long
frame Wandjina figures
and the Ranger uranium mine
as if they are one – old fuel
from an old country –
edifice mixing high
in ambient lushness of blood,
the vascular hum and spillage of references
devolving into bliss – purging
envy and astronomers during an eclipse,
bending carcasses splayed open
as if the internal organs
were of special interest, sweetbreads
for the Others; in short disc warps
spacetime attaches
itself and snaps back like the ochre
of textual rubber stretched out (this represents space –
and it's true, I borrow) at a distance,
ritualising victory perpetually
in a present tense, like Rick Deckard
amplifying self-importance
through Voight-Kampff Empathy,
asking who and what I am where
I've been and where I might go
as shining green the pleasant pastures extend
beyond the bitumen, the Vulgate.

FBI mysterium tremendum
and Chuck Harder's defending Bob on Chuck on,
for the people, on Chuck on, a mate
is a mate is a mate and identity is vernacular –
Bob answers, has answered questions
regarding the propulsion system of flying saucers,
223 grams of Luba Luft or a conventional aircraft,
red dirt getting into the works
wrecking four-wheel drives
edging down towards the coast
bringing rust to crops.

Half lives spread like blast zones
out in mallee territory
on the festive rifle range
where beer bottles
make temporary targets
and compounds spring up
overnight with specific intent,
charismatic leaders and suicide squads
garnish the flats. A burning man
dotes on colour and phallogocentric
enviro-vals while corpses congregate
on cutting tables – scalpel-edit
gimbols independently
from zero to 180 degrees
intelligent-looking Bob Lazar
knows a conspiracy when he sees it.

Brackish water distends veins
in the Nexus-6 person-Thing –
oh things I have seen:
nine discs in interconnecting hangars,
a corona discharge glowing blue hissing
with by-products out there in the paddocks
alone at night and not superstitious,
"spacetime" distorting the seasons,
words failing facts.

Mallee Meltdown

Smouldering mallee core
simultaneously bright
and dark hearted,
repository
of channelled aliens
out there with their tray-tops
and pick-ups, collecting vestiges,
wizened receptacles of combustible
hazards, old scrub knocked down
and abandoned, all arable now,
by the hearth, buried in the classifieds
of *The Western Farmer*, the woody pages
curling with the heat
walking into your body,
implanting
borderline territories
with its painstaking melt-
down

Visitant Eclogue

FARMER

Well, I said to the missus that something pretty odd
was happening out here, this being the third night
lights have appeared over the Needlings; and she
said stay clear Ben Rollins, stay clear, don't go
sticking your nose into something you don't understand.
And I said, well it's my place and if anything weird
is up I wanna know about it. And it's just starting
to dry off in these parts, and it's almost a fire risk.
The everlastings will be out soon and they'll dry
until they crinkle like cellophane in the hot
easterlies, and like a blowtorch they'd go up
taking the surrounding paddocks with them.
So here I am, *touched by your presence*, not quite
sure what to make of it but knowing that this
is as big as it gets, that death'll have nothing on it.

VISITANT

radiant inner heart countertracking epicycloidal
windrows and approaching harvest, as if to probe your body
like a contagion that'll never let you go,
corporate body politic, engraving crops
and stooking heretics, this our usufruct,
wickerman serving up the meek & generic
as vegetation names itself and the corpse
fills with a late shower, nomadic
emergent anticipation, toxic cloud of otherness
presence before authentic essay in defence
of time's minor fluctuations,
and we comprehend your gender,
missus as signifier to your gravelled utterance

FARMER

Now keep my missus out of it, she doesn't want
a bar of it – I've already made this clear. Hereabouts
it's mainly grain, though those offerings dotting the fields
in this brooding light are sheep that'll work in trails
down to the dam and struggle for shade or shelter beneath
a single tree. Around here used to be stands of mallee
and York Gum, though I'm not sure what the natives
call it. Yep, they were here before us,
though there's none around now so I can't help you there.

VISITANT

in family structure, as dialect wears out
and you claim ownership – down from the ship
we name and conquer, that's what you'd have us think,
to go your way and validate; scarifiers and hayrakes,
all aftermath and seed drilled to be ellipsed by grains
of superphosphate, expressionist and minimal
all at once, expanding tongues as if a place of worship
might spontaneously erupt, the face of a prophet
frowning in local stone, or grinning out of a piece
of imported fruit – the simplest is most exotic

FARMER

We've always been churchgoers, and I'm proud to say
that I'm an alderman; we've just got new bells
and they ring out through the valley like they're
of another world, and believe it or not, the congregation
has almost doubled in the last few weeks. I say
it's the bells but my wife reckons it's in the air,
that people feel depleted and need something
to absorb the emptiness. When pushed, she can't put
a finger on it. The minister has mentioned it in his sermons.

Down off the shoulder of the pink granite scarp

Down off the shoulder of the pink granite scarp
down in the rich soil where the roots run deep

crop circles appear with mathematical precision –
archetypal patterns that keep us wondering.

It's said they followed the people
from the Old Country – even after

the first clearing there was talk
of them, recurring every now and again

when the signs were right – when the harvest
was still some way off but the stems

of the long wheat varieties were fully
grown and the florescence of the crops

was at its peak. When the evenings
brooded bruised and red.

Soon they'll come...

Soon they'll come from the *Post*
and the *Truth*, the *West Australian*

and the local gazette, along with skeptics
and a brace of quacks all armed

with charts and instruments,
with metal detectors that transform

slivers of steel from a plough disc
into a discourse,

the weight of the heavens
now sits in fields as the salt

wells up and poisons
the fields.

Figures in a Paddock

In their wake the furrows,
partings in long grass,
burrs hell-darning their socks
like recovered memories.

Parallel to the fence – star pickets
mark depth, interlock mesh
letting the light and visuals
through, keeping the stock

in or out – like religious tolerance.
Down from the top-road to the creek,
arms akimbo, driven against
insect-noise, a breeze that should

be rustling up a performance.
Towards the dry bed, marked
by twists and shadow-skewed
river-gums, bark-texture

runs to colour like bad blood.
The sky is brittle blue,
foliage thin but determined:
colour indefinable beyond green.

They walk, and walking makes history.
And tracks. All machinery.
The paddock inclines. A ritual of gradients.
Ceremony. Massacre. Survey.

Divining

1

The Dry Multitudes
await the moisture –

the Diviner requests space,
loosening his collar.

Flies sap his strength,
dams of sweat are breached.

For many the hooked wire
refuses to move – for those

with the gift the feeling
is electric – an extension

of the body, a condensing
of Tractability and Energy.

2

An appetite for revelation –
the Unseen foiling the skeptics.

The wire taking control
and spinning madly, severing

shirt buttons, piercing the palm:
a stigmata of the rough edges.

And should waters erupt
and the course be tracked

the Dry Multitudes will turn
their backs – *a trick* they'll say,

and drinking deep in the waste's
red light, deny their thirst.

Harvest Time

Harvest time. Green fields
are now yellow,
most are still bare.
Some grow whiter,
the salt spreading further.
Hay bales like stele or crypts
or the residue of sun
in a sea of Horus's wheat
like stone ships friezing
sun-driven hydraulics,
the Green River running
darkly through the valley.
Totemic and primal
they lean into their shadows,
the blond floor of harvest
listless at their bases: these uprights
of antipodean stonehenges
temporal and mocking
the chthonic source of their
construction, commodities
that might explode with heat.
Cyclical and ephemeral
the hawk that dives for skinks,
and the cockatoos
perched like gargoyles –
eyes twisted to leers in masks.
The pattern of the machine
as it configures the paddock,
space contradicting
the brief time they persist sub-
consciously, rolling there
like chaotic empires
nearing the end of their days,
their situations as delicate
as the southern forest's
burnt orange haze, burnback
darkening catastrophe's fuel
like a dare, while nearby
stookers build ricks –

small offerings in fields
of obelisks gloating under
skies known for lightning,
the arsonist's glint.

The Road to Brookton
– *on the nature of memory*

(for John Kerrigan)

Back from England and fenland
we drive into the wheatbelt –
warm weather with the possibility
of a storm late in the day.
Or maybe it is cool, but warm
when compared with where
we've come from. Breaching
the Hills reservoirs and quarries
that feed the city, the excursion
reconstructs itself: everlastings
thick on roadsides broadcast
ethnographies and genealogies,
preparing for their seed-drop –
a dried persistent thought withering
and flaking like insect wings,
blown into the cautiously drying crop,
awaiting reconstitution. Movement
plays like a home video. The crops
and road-killed animals compile
as data – memory a webcrawler
hyperventilating references:
the yield looks okay from here,
that roo is still alive, gasping
for its last breath on the road's
gravel shoulder. There's gelatin
in this Kodak film, the sky's
too bright – glistens and gleams
like a cibachrome print.
They imported convict labour
late in the picture. Land rights
are up against it around here.
This State voted for succession
in the thirties. Was this one
of the roads resurfaced
with a Federal grant
during the Bicentennial Year?

A landmark defines itself –
granite outcrop or gnarled tree
in a very flat field fringed
by firebreaks. A UFO
was spotted hovering
over a field of gamenya wheat
last year. That's what we heard.
A little to the west the face
of Christ made an appearance
on a slab of stone – looking
mediaeval and European.
In a letter, on the telephone.
A scrap of gossip loose in memory.
It was, well... whatever.
Old technology. The new model
goes quickly out of date.
General Motors, Ford, Nissan.
I was reading Kropotkin
and thinking about Sidney Nolan.
We pass a beer can, a bullet-ridden
milepost, a broken fan-belt.
Radio waves lasso the culture.
The bright renderings – tarps on field bins,
on truck trailers – glow authentically
and we all have our say.
It's true, there's a waterbird
on the edge of the scrub
eating carrion. Dead sheep or roo.
It's the recollection that reeks.
It seemed logical at the time.
As if it had come to this, or that.
Between the properties Crown land
sticks out like a sore thumb.
The shells of burnt-out cars
confuse spotter planes and satellites.
A total fireban is close.
We listen for the news.
Overtaking, something is missed.
A dam brines beneath
the billowing stratosphere.
Bitumen wavers. Brookton
moves closer. A creek shadows

the highway – unmapped,
so there's hope for dialect.
The locals sleep away
their Sunday. Lightning stirs up
heat and recall grows oppressive.
All tenses and figures of speech
sulphur-crested white cockatoos
lift with Hitchcockian malevolence,
as if they shouldn't be there,
as if placid crows perched
on second-hand farm machinery
and rusted swings under wandoo trees
have conspired and incited them.
Caught out, struck down
by the suddenness of the storm,
we imagine that we're part of it,
that we belong there too,
knowing in the electric air
that this is not true.

Eclogue of the Eclipses

Though no longer near she casts her
shadow on the former
shadow of your darkness
constraining my day, and because of this
inclination thins opposition
like fire through undergrowth, an
obscuration of the light of the sun
while the moon wallows imagistically
in southern forests,
the waterbag in the plane
of the Ecliptic. Above the shearing-shed
conjecture casts her shadow
on the former like a theorem
not cooling as it should, passing
between earth and sun: it can,
the moon's orbit, intern
an animal magnetism. As it appears,
day-darkness lulls the bestiary
and we put on different faces,
the dead quiet muffling
even a work-hungry farmer.
From where you look
we remain un-haloed

It's the body you want
as it occurs with a new moon,
blown sheep fretting the obscuration
of internal lighting as it casts
her shadow on the latter:
because of inclination
it can thin opposition on the board,
and love becomes a lustful tally: but
it does not occur at every new moon
like calluses on my hands
burning casts of her shadow
on the former as handpieces whirr
together, in conjunction heating
and vibrating like oversexed monsters.

When the moon is the midday sun
viewed best from equatorial regions,
dead dark above thick layers
of cloud and exploitation.
Only at the time of full moons
can corrugated iron wipe out memory
as it passes between sun and earth

And when the moon is,
when the earth, passing
in the plane of the Ecliptic
between sun and moon
temporarily gives in
to a thin opposition that loses us;
the insistence of light
casting shadow onto the fringes
of wanting,   passing
between sun and earth;
like the John Deere tractor at night,
ploughing rain-softened earth,
clouds obscuring the likely
phenomena: it can, the moon's orbit,
appear bloody from where you look,
as, forced apart by science,
we seed the zodiac

ASPECTS OF THE PAGAN

The Fires Already Lit

> *'Mary reported that she was coming down in the early*
> *morning to find the fires already lit, and that it was*
> *the spirits responsible for the unexpected help...'*
> ALEX OWEN: The Darkened Room

When I come down in the early morning
and the fires have already been lit
I feel the sickness and return to bed.
Tom says, 'You're sick, I'll get you a cuppa.'
I don't say anything and he heads off
to the yellow kitchen. 'Here's your tea,'
he says, handing me our only cup
of Royal Doulton – I picked it up
for a song at the church fête years back.
For the rest of the day I lie stiff and pallid
in the darkened room. 'You shouldn't
have lit them fires if you're feeling crook,'
he says, scratching his chin. 'No,' I say,
'No, I shouldn't have lit them fires.'

Moving through the Range; and out there, the plains
(for Neil)

chrome and anatones high over saltpans discoid
like twilight zones of cultural sovereignty,
orbital carpet of wheedled scrub and thin–soiled grazing lands
where they might come, or might track
the ute like radar – you grow used to it, the vista
bluffing yellows and greens like camouflage
as water moves subversively,
and it's not a joke; a mere touch of the soil
rendering it potentially valuable to medicine,
as if we might map stars in the pavement
or create a false moonlanding, the breadth of land
shining under the passing satellite,
gloating beneath the shuttle
and its blinking focus; plethora
of banksias as old as the innards
of a mountain range where the gaps between peaks
are so broad nothing approaching a valley
lays demographic claim, and out there
the plains; concentration of visceral light
as granite outcrops heighten surrounding decay
and gravel roads are cut up, termites working the veins
within their mounds, as active as tense and always
in the second person, with a colourful local
telling another people's story as if it's his own
sans dislocation, because he's still there
and sees the lights when the tourists
are airconditioned or wrapped up warm
after cups of mulled wine; that he's been much
further away than they have come,
and that was no weather balloon
or experimental plane

The Spur

Being stuck out there in the middle of nowhere
it was natural they spent a lot of time with their
      neighbours the Hewitts, twenty
      miles down the road. Hollow
Point, a coastal town, was another hundred miles
further on. A dusty paddock of thin soil, their farm

was on the extreme edge of pastoral country,
so to get even a few dollars from it you
      had to work yourself to
      the bone; and as if caught
in a time warp there were few mod-cons – no TV,
no microwave, and only a radio to
      keep them both company.
A generator of sour temperament pushed

pale light into bare rooms at night. But it wasn't
an authentic portrait of "outback" endurance –
      they had money, lots of
      it invested in stocks
and bonds, mining futures. This scene, circa nineteen
thirties, appealed to them in a perverse sort of
      way. They almost liked it.
The Hewitts, who were genuinely poor – or 'broke'

as their wealthier neighbours preferred to describe
it – hated the place with a vengeance. They'd been
      there for almost twelve years –
      having moved up from the
coast to make a go of it, thinking nothing could
be as hard as a bitchy town a day's driving
      from the city. They were
wrong. When the new people moved up a ray of hope

illuminated their burnt horizons. Soon they spent
weekends in each other's company. Pete Hewitt's
        spur toe had broken the
        ice. Noticing it one day
Sarah had gasped out loud. Pete, bare foot stuck out in
front of him laughed, 'helps me keep a firm grip on the
        planet!' They'd laughed with him.
All of them were drinkers. And they drank to get drunk.

And with all that space they could do what they wanted.
They had their own laws, their own codes of behaviour.
        Their parties continued
        well on into Sarah's
pregnancy – pregnancy had its own mysteries.
It was a bitter winter. Little rain but dire
        cold. The scant crops died off.
They tried to reseed but it was too late. Disease

hit the flocks and sheep dropped off in their hundreds.
The days were spent collecting mallee roots to burn.
        Peter cursed poverty.
        Sarah wanted to speak
but was pinched hard by her husband – 'they mustn't
know,' he told her when their friends had gone home. 'We live
        like them and that's why we
are friends, we've got to keep it to ourselves.' The child

clawed hard at the core of her belly. A home birth.
A Sister came from town and stayed for a week. 'Who's
        got one of these in your
        family?' she asked light-
heartedly, squeezing the baby's spur toe. A crow
laughed and a flight of galahs headed south. Sarah
        didn't look up. It was
bitterly cold and the Sister didn't approve.

'Not the best place to bring up a child.' But she left
with a smile on her face when they paid her twice her
        regular fee without
        a grimace. Asked later
if anything had seemed out of place, she said, 'things
seemed really fine, except for that spur.' The neighbours
        dropped in regularly
even though they lived twenty miles away, always

on hand to help out, keep the mother company,
travel out to the wells and windmills to make sure
    things were functioning
    smoothly. She'd heard it was
a tough year out there – no rain, no crop, dead sheep – but they
seemed happy enough. 'No reason to go that far,
    to end it that way. And
money wasn't a problem. It was strange seeing

them stretched out like that – I'd swear there wasn't a mark
on them. These blokes in suits asked me heaps of questions
    and others in plastic
    costumes blocked the gravel
roads. I didn't mention it but I touched Sarah's
cheek and the tips of my fingers burnt like acid.'

Exotica at Lake Joondalup

(for Ato Quayson)

Lake Joondalup – satellite city –
shaping suburbs laid out
like empty circulatory systems,
blood traffic-hungry,
buttressed walls and formatted
ground/lake, stele squeezed
tight together, industry's
treated pine setting root
in little Arcadia – a plastic module
Swedish look, equipment
as exact as folly, highly
photogenic lakes used as backdrops,
birds mounted
over shopping centres.
Spiritual ladies stretch palms
towards Snyderesque
parrots, mystical glow
suppressing muscular twitches
within neat oval faces
retaining fluttered states of plural bliss,
dense flights of crows
invading space, as if to lift
or break sacred bonds
of Nature, avoiding
charismatics
in scrub that's close
to the lake's edge, a fringe
through which birds
move carelessly.
Oblivious, though out of reach,
white-faced heron and egrets
defend territory silently,
quick slice of light knifing water,
prey darting shadows
of grave movements.
Paperbark groves cluster.
A small fish loses its head.

Paperbarks skinless
ringbarked flesh bone-like ivory
stripped back pentagram
red paint and a litany of bottles,
Angel's Trumpet decaying
earthmoving equipment
poised on boundaries forced
into one another's flesh – a defensive
reaction against depth,
against vast mounds of water
beneath dirt tracks
ploughed by yellow cars.
The car a trope, a giraffe
or Nile Cow perfectly
yellow in yellow light,
post-colonial jibes
strangely Skeltonic
as precisely doggerel rhythms,
plastic oil containers,
spray drums from market gardens
rotting in ground
hesitantly peaty.
Deeply historic unearthing
will be sealed beneath
a cap of asphalt and concrete,
only power lines
humming alternative lifeforce.
Zoo-bound giraffe
preserving late twentieth-century
expediency – Crosse's
imported exotica, lacking
rosetta stones between Victorian England/
Joondalup

Aspects of the Pagan

'there/ blossoms precious flesh and after'

we call it a Thursday, harvesting lust
in the public of trees, investigating
the drop into the black hole of verdure
in Italy and Upper Palatinate: Nider, Friuli,
Kemnnat: Ember day souls in purgatory
on display, the Carlo Ginzberg(ian)
furious horde, women leading with
generous thighs, journeying motif
under the direction of Abundia-Satia-
Diana-Perchta, impervious to pricks
the Ember Days of Christmas, those hordes
of early deaths or those as precise
as the mathematics of crop circles
in the glades of Norman Lindsay

in the glades of Norman Lindsay
the red shift shows receding galaxies
of attendant sycophants, the halls
of Australian poetry, only annular
eclipses possible in this short of breath
salutation, the dark eyed copse sullen
in snow glowing as inversion the fields
of summer grain and exaltation as the last
circle is cut and fed into the waiting hopper
into the tardis belly of the little grassbird
and in turn the belly of a goshawk or near
the brooding wetlands that of the swamp harrier,
that just below the exuberant trappings
surfaces echo like coronas, the yawn of lust

surfaces echo like coronas, the yawn of lust
a dark herald on the heaths and commons
of enjambment | considered as backdrop
to the *goings-on* and dragging of chains
and obelisks through particularly verdant
chunks of scrubland, the Georgic bounty
of a new arcadia laboured in the glossies
and saturating television: as if in looking up
they'd be blinded, transfixed and burnt
to the tender core, as embellishment
or reduction in the wickedary as returning
the small sweet wonders have us lapping
at the vanishing fragrance, the pressings
of a drunken strain, an allergy to pollen

of a drunken strain, an allergy to pollen
they wedded gaily around the sundial:
a skull-capped wedding in the overflowing
gardens, a skull-capped garden as the oldest
ritual, and despite the searing post-ecliptic
sun drawing driven sap greenly against
the hessian backdrop, you wander by
and are welcomed, the plosive voice of festive
luring, as if the skin of decorum were
stripped − écorché − the beautiful flesh
vigorously working against the designs
of history, that language works against
a repetition, though seems lacking
in the dying breath, the riot of roses

in the dying breath, the riot of roses
clans against a precocious <u>talent</u>} a-drift
the seamy escapades of romantic jest,
the forlorn mutability of lush nights
on the rockface, high in the imperative
alps, or south, among the peaks
of the Stirling Ranges, where voices
confuse location and the heady fall
to forgotten places: a murmur
of this mysterious and awful doubt
in the glades of Norman Lindsay:
surfaces echo like coronas, the yawn of lust,
of a drunken strain, an allergy to pollen
in the dying breath, the riot of roses

Akbar

The swarming things swarm in the wall space as heavy
as liquid concrete the flawed wall fast collapses,
spilling out all is unclean in the bright sunlight
as they dash crazily into dusk, carcass on
seed so sown but wet seed and carcass as unclean
as geckoes hesitate over Leviticus
and then Samuel, guilt offering of five golden
tumours and five golden mice as the ark comes back
to solve the ills of plague, cantankerous sheep with
their stomachs bloated, the salt scars and the torn creeks,
the dozer on its rippled tracks cutting a new
road through the last stand of trees and the mice bursting
up out of paddocks and into silos and through
hessian and polyurethane sacks and into
houses – testing cupboards and children's beds, the cats
sick of the flesh of mice so satiated they
run scared from the seething blankets, the kids filling
holes with buckets of water and blasting ratshot,
crazy with buckets and lengths of polythene pipe,
every sheet of corrugated iron bubbling
like molten zinc, galvanised under the harsh white
moonlight, a collusion of seasons, the climate
just right, the parthenogenesis of brash top soil,
the tunnels the vessels carrying rich sustenance
to a shrivelling surface. As now ideas too
full for allotted space spill into the nervous
system like mercury, thought the stimulant to
a flurry of possibilities, a smiting
plague that eats away at the store of plump seed grain
collected from the fullest heads in the densest
crops on ground rich with nurturing – that no planning
or safeguards could prevent such a dark collusion
of seasons, of heat, of moisture, of a bumper
year it's avowed...but that's after the trap's been sprung!

So now the mice moving in their millions devour
with one mind, consuming the body of the earth,
squeezing through its pores, filling even space between
particles, until they become the one body,
the akbar of myth, the unclean creature that is
the flesh, the breath; that is the progeny of dirt.

nature morte: Oh Rhetoric!
(for John Tranter)

Calls for clarity
suggest the breakdown
or rediscovery of a market
like horrible workers
following Rimbaud
as he moves through and out
of the post-modern
work ethic, meaning just hanging there
like an island buoyed by dense air,
as the earth revolves unsecured
beneath.
The masters leave studios
& paint only for personal
gratification – horrible workers
keeping the studios going,
contracting art to a single flourish
of pen or brush. Like Cicciolina
being the model for everything
in the glossy magazine apartments
of *meta-kitsch*. Or Elle Macpherson
saying you should only read
what you've written yourself.
Or Christo hiding dead art
beneath swathes of wrapping.
On the Island of Doctor
Moreau the animal-humans
animate analogies & moralise
as we take our medicine.
Taking the cure means
making it suffer. Metaphor
is the only way of saying something
plain & simple & as we turn full circle
towards Babel Fowler becomes a kind of
trendy gibberish. In
Giacomo Balla's
Dynamism of a Dog on a Leash
we notice the energy
of a still in which Balla

delights in the simultaneity
of deprivation. Innovation
is the fraudulent usage
of an established
method of discussion
on the nature of intent
& inspiration
only because there's a market.
We might still be drawn to expression
without a means of exchange
but it's unlikely we'd be pushed
to validate it. But that's
in a perfect world where your indulgence
wouldn't bother anyone a damn.
That if you didn't work you'd starve
alone. A doctor tells the story
of a suicide who survived
just long enough fully to comprehend
the totality of pain. He'd drunk toilet cleaner
& then changed his mind.
Like the late twentieth century.
There's no need to refer to *particular*
incidents to make this a political poem.
I can analogise by using the Island
of Doctor Moreau & prompting the reader
to consider the tyrannies of science,
which is a euphemism
for The Law Giver is dead.
The Ipecacuanha like a UFO fixation.
In the House of Pain Moreau said: 'You
forget all that a skilled vivisector
can do with living things.'
Here, if you wish
for an absolute kind of illumination
you must of course
read the book. I have read the book.
A lot of my friends are writers.
Many are venerated by their peers
& would be considered to have good taste
in things literary. I write a poem & hand it around.
Some praise it as the best thing I've written,
other suggest I return to the draft-board,

others that I scrap it & take a rest.
I consider that *the best thing*
you've written might not mean much
if deep down they think that the rest
of your stuff is pretty lousy.
Even their judgements
have different meanings
depending on how they tell me & how I listen.
Style doesn't change, but styles do.
I once led into a poem with a quote
from Brodsky: 'Everything has its limit,
including sorrow.' I read the poem. It's titled
'Trans-celluloid Vision'. I consider why
the quote is used? The poem is in three
parts and the last stanza reads: 'Everything has its limit –
the train slowing, the journey
almost complete. Relief
borders on sorrow.
I lose track of the plot,
embracing the platform.' In the <u>light</u>
of the rest of the poem *this* is a little "tacked on".
It is a poem about a fragmenting relationship;
a kind of lament.
But this doesn't really come through
so it can't ~~really~~ be about that.
I haven't guided the reader.
through italicising 'can't'
to make my intention clear(er).
My problems continue(d)
with a second reading
& I suggest(ed)
it's another of those I gave up on but wasn't able
to get rid of.
Years later & I'm at it again.
The first line of section 1 (View from a train)
reads 'The curve of the track/betrays the engine.'
I remember the train going from Sydney to Melbourne.
That the <u>mystery of movement</u> was lost when
the engine appeared out of the window. I think it was
raining & the atmosphere was 'surreal'. But this
is not my word, it comes from somewhere else.
The poem continues: 'Moisture

90

trapped within the double-paned window
makes liars of manufacturers claiming
air-tight security. I stare past the frame
of lacquered wood & outside the day
is cinematographic. Flickering
from reel to reel until the credits
show the names of logging & catering companies,
trucking & management industries.'
The second stanza turns against the first:
'A green desert. Sheep moving slowly
through viscous paddocks, water pooling
like blood. Dry country stranded
on the backbone of grey granite.
A washed sunset emphasises
the sharp teeth of a retreating city.'
I recall being dissatisfied with the 'washed
sunset' – maybe 'brooding' or 'harsh'
or some other more active adjective?
But it was the bitterness of sorrow
that intrigued & this disparate
image stuck. In the dissection
of the corpse of this poem
I recall Lyn Hejinian
telling me how she'd gone to watch
autopsies with Mike Patton,
the lead singer of *Faith No More*.
I wouldn't have mentioned Mike but his music
has always interested me & if he hadn't been
on world tour I'd have tried to solicit
material for the literary journal I edit.
Lyn said
that in this de-sensitized environment
(actually that's my word, I can't remember
what she said specifically but its effect
on me was to suggest this) the body
wasn't that frightening.
I think she held a liver.
I asked if it was like a collection of artefacts
being removed carefully from a tomb.
I think she laughed.
But it might not have
been a comfortable laugh. The second section

of my poem is entitled: 'The Cat
& The Canary or The Absence Of Sorrow
Accompanying A Belated Reading
Of The Millionaire's Will: A Reconstruction
To Help Pass The Time' So, it's <u>sorrow</u>
by association. In <u>true</u> post-modern spirit
I digress into commentary on a 1927 b & w
horror film. Somewhere in there there's
the influence of Tranter. I'm tossing up
whether to "background" this piece.
No, I'll quote it in full & then elaborate,
simply noting that the long lines
do not best capture the short subtitles
that accompany silent movies but <u>do</u> suggest
the notion of linear narrative. Maybe
as you read the long-lined version
you can also visualise how it would
look were it segmented, chopped up:
'The late night silent classic for the real buffs.
Shot in '27. The director died two years later
Of blood poisoning. The screen throws a double image,
The UHF aerial failing, or the ghost of the director
Fermenting 'in-camera' with age. He has the cast
Lip-synching their way through a reading
Of an eccentric millionaire's will in a house
That his ghost has occupied for twenty years.
There is Mammy Patient, Susan & the famous
West Diamonds, Annabelle, Paul, & The Lawyer.
GHOSTS! The portrait falls to the floor.
Mammy inks her brow. The will
Mentions a distant relative & demands
Sanity. The lawyer disappears. The murderer –
Claw-fingered & with nails like razors
Is seen only by Susan, who must PROVE
Her sanity! The doctor with peculiar hands
Arouses suspicion. There's a moth in the safe
Though it's not been opened for twenty years!
And who hired the imposter asylum warder
Who's hunting a madman who tears
His victims as a cat does a canary?'
Strangely, this section stops here.
No ~~witty~~ line that might hint at resolution.

If the title is considered we might
reflect on the ruthlessness
of the participants.
An allegory of the twentieth century.
Or of the human condition generally?
It's been noted that the last stanza
of the final section
seems a little "tacked on".
But in the light of the second section maybe
it's a pretty *obvious* conclusion?
Part 3 ('Solarization – a celebration') reads:
'Sunrise.
My mind blank.
Spencer Gore's painting
The Icknield Way 1912
appears stereoscopic
on my glasses, or so
I'm told. A geometric
almost tabular sky
registers through a film
of brilliant light
as the train celebrates
the approaching city's
solarization.
The sky inflects
& organises fancy:
the landscape bright,
explosive, threatens
to ignore the script.'
'Organises fancy' – it reminds **me**
of a review by James Dickey
on John Ashbery's first
collection of poetry.
I can't remember what he said exactly
but he hated the book.
I tracked the book down
& thought it was great.
But then I like Ashbery{'s poetry}.
There's something about his use of weirs,
I think.
I'm reminded of Vasari
talking of Leonardo

saying that he could find no living model
for the features for his head of Christ,
so it was best left incomplete. It existed in my files
as a kind of still life,
as a piece of dead nature
waiting for clarity,
hinting at de–
composition.

Glare

(for Xavier Pons)

As if whipped up by the water itself,
or molecules of air coated with glass –
the sun fragmented and stuck inside,
frantic to get out, or the brightness
inside your head turned all the way up.
Full blown, making a place snow-bound
and twenty below conceptually the same
as a space burnt to dunes of white sand.
In painting this universal portrait
of landscape – the deflection
of light off a pond in the Tuileries,
or snowburn from a drift in Alberta,
or the car lifted on the Nullarbor
and a whole family probed by aliens
(the car has been impounded
in America, the case is pending),
or the intensity of solarium hills
on a forty-degree day near Sydney –
all fit comfortably in the same frame,
without frontiers or contraries.
We must paint with the essence
of place, or what illuminates
memories of having travelled
out of our bodies. In the light of day
it's the intensity of sight, or resistance
to glare, that counts as constant.
And bright the implanted lights –
the *son et lumière* of a radio telescope,
the brilliance of the platinum Metre –
so bright we dare not look.

Ascension

I stripped down to my underpants and folded my clothes neatly
and placed them on the floor at the base of the bed, along with my
new pump-up Reeboks; the others did the same

I placed the tape of The Director's transference composition
in the Walkman and inserted the earpieces, lay down on the bed
with the tape player next to me; the others did the same

The Director walked amongst us touching our foreheads, pushing
the play button – it was as if he'd touched our souls – already
we'd become as one though I felt guilty because it touched me
inside, it had been so long; I can't speak for the others

And he placed a capsule in our mouths and we bit down as we'd
been instructed – the window being so narrow, a matter of minutes,
but he moved swiftly and deftly, as always; as a body we'd rise
to the Mothership as it swept past in its arc; we'd rise as one

The Director would follow close behind, delivered by his own hand
– prophet, holder of the dates, the co-ordinates, banker and father
and keeper of the texts; the only one

The computers and our brilliant technology would remain,
our website maintained by believers who'd lacked the strength
to make the leap forward, who'd be waiting for the next time,
waiting for a new Director to lead them into the sun,
to full knowledge, immortality; oneness